LIVES OF IRISH ARTISTS

# O'CONOR

*Roderic O'Conor*
*1860-1940*

PAULA MURPHY

# O'CONOR

*Roderic O'Conor
1860 - 1940*

PAULA MURPHY

THE NATIONAL GALLERY OF IRELAND
IN ASSOCIATION WITH
TOWN HOUSE, DUBLIN

Published in 1992 by

Town House

42 Morehampton Road

Donnybrook

Dublin 4

for The National Gallery of Ireland

British Library Cataloguing in Publication Data

Murphy, Paula

Roderic O'Conor, 1860–1940. — (Lives of Irish Artists Series)

I. Title II. Series

759.2915


ISBN: 0-948524-38-3

Cover: *The Farm at Lezaven* 1894 (National Gallery of Ireland)

Title page: *Self portrait* 1903 (National Gallery of Ireland)

Managing editor: Treasa Coady

Series editor: Brian P Kennedy (NGI)

Text editors: Elaine Campion, Bernie Daly

Colour origination: The Kulor Centre

Design concept: Q Design

Printed in Hong Kong

# CONTENTS

Paula Murphy is a lecturer in the history of art in University College Dublin. She has a particular interest in Irish art and has published on Irish sculpture and painting of the nineteenth and twentieth centuries. She has also presented a video examining aspects of Irish painting in the National Gallery of Ireland.

For many years Roderic O'Conor was recognised popularly in his native Ireland due to his association with Paul Gauguin. This association gave O'Conor considerable status among Irish artists. At the same time many would have considered O'Conor's art not quite of the standard of that of his more famous friend. But O'Conor has now emerged from the shadow of Gauguin as Ireland's most important early modernist painter, a colourist of exciting dimensions.

Not confined by insularity, nor by Irishness, Roderic
O'Conor was more European than many of his contemporaries. He worked for most of his life in France. While his initial training was in Ireland, his real awakening was a result of his contact with post-impressionist art. It was almost a requirement of artists at this time that they should undertake some study abroad, but they generally maintained their Irish identity and returned to work in Ireland. O'Conor was more of a free spirit, in touch with modern approaches to painting on the continent, and seemingly aware that national boundaries were a barrier to freedom of expression.

O'Conor arrived in France in the 1880s, at a time when the impressionist painters, who for more than a decade had been the subject of hostile criticism, were beginning to receive favourable comments. Criticism was now being directed at the post-impressionists, particularly Vincent van Gogh, the man who would have the most marked influence on O'Conor in his early expressive explorations.

# EARLY TRAINING

Born in 1860 at Milton in County Roscommon, Roderic O'Conor, one of six children, was the son of well-to-do parents. His father's legal career obliged the family to move to Dublin when O'Conor was five. While his early education may have been in the family home, he was later sent to the Benedictine College at Ampleforth in Yorkshire. In 1875, during his second year at the school, his younger brother Joseph died from diphtheria, and O'Conor was the only member of the family present. This traumatic incident, when he was still only fifteen, must have drawn O'Conor into early maturity.

Ampleforth was strong in the classical, literary and artistic areas of education, and O'Conor emerged from this background with an excellent academic record. He decided to study art and enrolled at the Dublin Metropolitan School of Art in January 1879. O'Conor's early training followed the recognised academic system both at the Metropolitan School and at the Royal Hibernian Academy where he studied for one year. He was a prize-winner on a number of occasions, drawing from the antique and from the live model. He also believed in the theory of furthering one's knowledge of art through close study of the work of other artists and he spent regular periods of time copying old master paintings in the National Gallery of Ireland. Of the group of artists studying with him in Dublin at the time, O'Conor was the most adventurous. Towards the close of the century, when George Russell, a fellow student at the Metropolitan School, was beginning to recognise the importance of developments in art taking place outside of Ireland, Roderic O'Conor was already immersed in them.

O'Conor's path towards modernism took him from Dublin to France, via Antwerp. Was this simply the recognised study trip abroad, or was O'Conor seeking to escape from the conservative environment of an art scene that attempted to focus on Irishness, whose Royal Irish Academy, for example, found native subject matter by far the most acceptable? In choosing the Académie Royale des Beaux-Arts at Antwerp, O'Conor was following in the footsteps of Walter Osborne. During his year at the Académie, 1883/4, he undertook a course entitled *Natuur*, drawing and painting from nature. The classes were taught by Charles Verlat who opened O'Conor's eyes to the use of more vivid colours in painting and to a more vigorous approach to the application of those colours on canvas. Both of these elements would later be reinforced through his contact with the art of van Gogh.

Paris in the 1880s was the exhibition centre of modern developments in art. The impressionists had been exhibiting their own work independently since 1874, thereby breaking the stranglehold of the Salon, the official exhibition platform in the city. Their final group exhibition in 1886 was less a last impressionist show and more a revelation of new trends in art. Neo- and post-impressionist artists, not yet labelled as such, were exploring new techniques in painting and new depths in subject matter, beyond the surface approach of impressionism. This was the scene into which Roderic O'Conor arrived and it is interesting to see how he merged aspects of impressionism and post-impressionism in his art.

O'Conor studied in Paris with the portrait artist Carolus-Duran, who encouraged the expressive technique of fusing drawing and painting. He also recommended a study of the paintings of the Spanish artist Velázquez, who, in the seventeenth century, had painted with an expressive sketchiness. At the same time O'Conor frequented the premises of art dealers in Paris, in search of contemporary work, and there he would have seen canvases by Seurat, Gauguin and van Gogh. It is possible that O'Conor met van Gogh at this stage, just before the latter's departure for Arles, and he would certainly have seen his work exhibited at the Salon des Indépendants in Paris in 1889 and 1890.

O'Conor underwent a somewhat similar experience to van Gogh in relation to the metropolis. He had absorbed a variety of new ideas in the city, but had to leave it in order to express them in his own work. Towards the end of the 1880s O'Conor moved south of

cont. p25

# ILLUSTRATIONS

PLATE 1

Breton Girl 1903

13

*Pl 1*

The Breton woman was a subject much explored by artists in the second half of the nineteenth century, offering a primitive directness unattainable in the big city. The traditional clothing provided interesting possibilities of contrasts and patterning. In this statuesque image O'Conor captures a sadness that is hypnotic to the viewer.

Oil on canvas; 91.5 x 73.6 cm
Hugh Lane Municipal Gallery of Modern Art, Dublin

PLATE 2

---

Between the Cliffs, Aberystwyth *c* 1885

*Pl 2*    Nothing is known of O'Conor visiting Wales, but th

*painting is of interest for its vigorous technique, an*

*because it reveals his early approach to landsca*

*imagery.*

Oil on panel; 24.1 x 32.4 cm

*14*    National Gallery of Ireland

PLATE 3

eld of Corn, Pont Aven 1892

*15*

*Pl 3*    **A**lthough *O'Conor moved to Pont Aven to join the community of artists working in the spirit of Gauguin, the strength of his own expressive powers meant that Gauguin's influence is rarely evident in his work. Here the richness of the yellow corn, intensified by the surrounding tapestry of colour, reveals something of this strength.*

Oil on canvas; 38.2 x 38 cm
Ulster Museum, Belfast

PLATE 4

The Farm at Lezaven 1894

*Pl 4*    The farm at Lezaven had served as an artists' studi*
*for some years before 1894 when O'Conor painted it*
*O'Conor probably worked in this studio but hi*
*landscapes were more likely painted out of doors, usin*
*nature as a vehicle for exploring colour. Strident an*
16    *very expressive strokes of the brush, combined with*
*vibrant contrasting colours, reveal the influence of va*
*Gogh.*

Oil on canvas; 72.4 x 92.7 cm
National Gallery of Ireland

PLATE 5

Boulevard Raspail *c* 1905

*Pl 5*     **M**ontparnasse *was one of the artists' quarters in Paris and it was here that O'Conor had his studio, not far from the Boulevard Raspail. Cityscapes and night scenes are unusual in his work and have an ominous, uneasy note not present in his landscapes.*

17

Oil on canvas; 54.3 x 65.4 cm
Hugh Lane Municipal Gallery of Modern Art, Dublin

PLATE 6

Reclining Nude before a Mirror 1909

18

Pl 6     **O**'*Conor aspired towards a greater understanding of*

*art by studying old master works, especially those of*

*Velázquez. The Spanish painter had created in The*

*Rokeby Venus (National Gallery, London) an image of*

*the goddess before a mirror, a sophisticated back view*

*which inspired O'Conor to a more* intimiste *interpretation*

*of the subject, sketchy in its treatment.*

Oil on canvas; 53.3 x 73.7 cm
National Gallery of Ireland

PLATE 7

Girl Reading *c* 1910

*Pl 7*   T*he interior of O'Conor's studio in Paris was full of still-life objects. On one occasion he painted, in a riot of colour, a girl immersed in a book, totally oblivious to her surroundings. This could hardly be described as a portrait; O'Conor's technique is loose and he is not interested in details.*

20

Oil on canvas; 54.6 x 64.8 cm
Private collection

PLATE 8

ris 1913

*Pl 8*  In the south of France, in Cassis, O'Conor's strident
early technique softened under the influence of the fauve
and the nabis painters. His still-life imagery always
concerns itself with compositional arrangement, and in
this work Japanese elements, long popular in France, are
still visible. Nonetheless this image has a passionate  *21*
intensity rarely seen in O'Conor's work.

Oil on canvas; 61 x 50.2 cm
Tate Gallery, London

PLATE 9

Still Life 1924

22

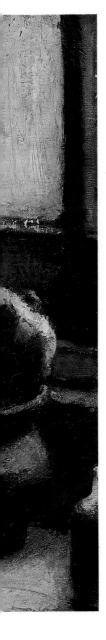

This still life was purchased from the artist by the critic Roger Fry on a visit to Paris. O'Conor was popular with several art critics because he had first-hand information of painting before the turn of the century and was au fait with developments that were taking place in Paris at the time. This work shows an awareness of the classical revival in the 1920s.

23

Oil on canvas;
57.2 x 45.7 cm
Courtauld Institute Galleries, London

PLATE 10

Torremolinos 1935

24

Pl 10   O'Conor was seventy-three when he married René
Honta and moved to Spain for almost two years. Hi
paintings of Torremolinos are amongst his last work
and, though quite different to his Brittany work, reveal
similar treatment of the landscape as those painted i
Cassis twenty years earlier.

Oil on board; 38.1 x 45.7 cm
Private collection

Paris to Grez, in the vicinity of Barbizon and the forest of Fontainebleau, where so many French landscape painters had worked in the first half of the century. O'Conor had been preceded in Grez by other Irish artists, in particular John Lavery with whom he had recently become acquainted. It was from here that he first sent work for exhibition at the Salon des Indépendants in 1889.

## Brittany and Gauguin

While the new developments taking place in art could be viewed in exhibitions in Paris, the work was largely produced elsewhere in France. Post-impressionist artists worked beyond the great cultural centre in more primitive environments, one of the most popular being Brittany, which towards the end of the century was being advertised as an artist's paradise. Roderic O'Conor arrived at the tiny Breton village of Pont Aven in 1892. Since the 1860s artists had succumbed to the magical and picturesque charm of this still incredibly pretty village, attracted by the somewhat exotic wildness of its primitive environment. Here they experienced an intoxicating sense of freedom not felt in the big city, and there was the added attraction that they could live very cheaply.

It was at Pont Aven that Paul Gauguin developed  
*cloisonnist* style of painting, that of rendering form  
areas of flat rich colour, emphatically outlined. If th  
appeared to be a simplification in terms of execution, l  
interest in superimposing memory and imagination  
nature made his work more enigmatic. A community  
artists established itself around Gauguin in Pont Ave  
but when O'Conor arrived their leader had already l  
for the South Sea Islands. Gauguin's spirit and sty  
however, remained all-pervasive.

O'Conor explored the Breton subject in a mo  
expressive way than earlier Irish artists who had work  
in Brittany. His figure paintings from this period a  
overtly Breton in character, his subjects often weari  
typical Breton dress, and he captures something of t  
haughty dignity of the primitive peasant nature. F  
landscapes, though images of particular locations in t  
environs, are less specifically Breton, and it is in many  
these works that O'Conor reveals the influence of v  
Gogh rather than of Gauguin. His method of applyi  
paint with strident, directional strokes of the brus  
often making use of a stripe-technique, and employi  
intense, even vibrant colour, ally him to van Gogh. V  
Gogh, however, explored the hidden depths of natu  
O'Conor's explosive landscape images contain no me  
than surface expression. Neither does he conce  
himself much with the imaginative possibilities prese  
in the work of Gauguin. It is in this period that O'Cor

most manifests the dual influences of impressionism and post-impressionism. If his technique reveals post-impressionist methods, its ultimate expression relates more to impressionism.

O'Conor spent much of this period at Pont Aven but he also travelled to other places in Brittany, to Paris, and even back to Ireland after his father's death in October 1893. He was an infrequent visitor to Ireland throughout his life and seems to have been totally unconcerned with his roots. On the death of his father he inherited the family estate in Roscommon, which obliged him to maintain contact, mostly by letter, and his subsequent landlord status gave him considerable financial independence. His trips to Paris were usually connected with the exhibition of his work there, where it was hung in the company of artists like Gauguin and Serusier, Vuillard and Bonnard, and many more.

O'Conor was finally to meet Gauguin, who returned to France from Tahiti in 1894. Gauguin paid a brief visit to Brittany and was impressed with the work of the Irish painter. He suggested that O'Conor return with him to the South Seas, and even went so far as to write in a letter that he was taking an Irishman back to Tahiti with him. It was a crucial decision for O'Conor. Gauguin had a powerful and dominant personality, and very specific ideas about painting, all of which had been manifest in his relationship with van Gogh in the course of his short sojourn at Arles in 1888. Had O'Conor's curiosity encouraged him to accompany Gauguin on the return voyage, he would probably have remained forever in the shadow of this more innovative artist, and it is unlikely that he would have progressed to the loose and delicate expressive work that was to become the hallmark of his particular *fauve* style. His own personality, which seems to have been independent and forceful, may have been the deciding factor. In any event, O'Conor declined the offer. Although he remained firmly attached to Brittany and did not make a complete break with the area until 1904, his most interesting work from this period was done before the turn of the century.

*28*

❧

## BACK IN PARIS

O'Conor spent much of the remainder of his life in or relatively close to Paris, and he also visited Italy, Spain and the south of France. In the early twentieth century Paris continued to be one of the most exciting centres of art in Europe, scarcely rivalled by Munich or Berlin. Exhibitions in Paris between 1905 and the outbreak of the First World War revealed several new developments in art: *fauve*, cubist and abstract. It was at this point that Picasso and Matisse were taking centre stage. Although O'Conor certainly did not favour all of these styles, he was nonetheless at the heart of what was taking place.

One of his first moves in the city was to involve himself in the very vibrant café society. He rented a studio in Montparnasse, an area of Paris much favoured by artists, and frequented the local Chat Blanc, where in the now established tradition of the Parisian art world, a group of artists and writers, including critics and theorists, gathered regularly to debate the issues of the day. This group was mainly English speaking, although some French artists, including the sculptor Rodin, occasionally showed up. One of the group, Somerset Maugham, who owned several of O'Conor's paintings, seems to have felt an intense animosity towards the Irishman, and he characterised him unfavourably in one of his novels, *Of Human Bondage*.

It was at this stage that O'Conor began to receive recognition amongst his peers and was invited to serve on the selection jury of the Salon d'Automne in 1908, where he was in a position to pass judgement on the work of artists such as Modigliani, Braque and Matisse. This role, however, left him with a certain distaste for the jury system. His official involvement with the Salon coincided with the brief high-point of *fauve* painting, a style that would soon begin to manifest itself in his own art. Many of the *fauve* artists had painted in the south of France, particularly at Cassis, where Matisse, Derain and Vlaminck had already spent some time. This may have been O'Conor's impetus to rent a villa there in 1913.

Cassis is a small, attractive fishing village close to

Marseilles. Here O'Conor painted for much of the year
reimmersing himself in landscape imagery. If hi
brushwork was heavy, emphatic and expressionis
during the Brittany years, it became gentle, loose and
sketchy in the southern light. Images of the villa and it
surroundings glow, not with the intense burning heat of
the Mediterranean, but with a rather more acceptabl
level of Provençal warmth.

❧

# A LATE MARRIAGE

O'Conor had featured women as subject matter i
his paintings throughout his career, from the ver
specific studies of Breton women, through several nud
paintings, to the informal renderings of seated o
reclining figures. Many amongst this last category hav
the appearance of portraits, but they remai
unidentified, with accompanying and unrevealing titl
such as *Woman in White* or *Seated Woman*. It
probably the case that these were not expressions o
individuality and that the figure was to have no mo
importance in the image than would still-life objects. I
one such painting, however, a half-length seated figu
entitled *The Green Blouse*, the woman can be identifi
as Renée Honta.

Honta was O'Conor's favourite model, later his mistress and pupil, and ultimately his wife. Born in 1894, she was thirty-four years younger than O'Conor. They had known one another for many years before they married in Paris in 1933, after which they moved to Torremolinos in Spain where they lived for almost two years. Before leaving France they purchased a house in the Maine-et-Loire region, just south of Brittany, and they returned to live there in 1935. Honta at this stage must *31* have taken on her final role as resident nurse, because O'Conor, who had experienced several bouts of ill health already, became increasingly unwell in the remaining years of his life. He may have hoped to produce further landscape images, exploring this new region of his adopted country, but he actually did very little painting in these last years. Roderic O'Conor died in his eightieth year at his home in Nueil-sur-Layon on 18 March 1940. His wife Renée survived him by almost fifteen years.

## THE MAN AND HIS ART

O'Conor has been described as a formidable person. Moving for most of his life in a circle of painters and writers, an environment of animated and stimulating debate, he seems rarely to have aired his views on art and could not be considered a theorist. He was capable of being withdrawn and solitary, and certainly the self portraits and photographs reveal an air of guarded distance. Although there were other Irish artists in Brittany and Paris at the same time as O'Conor, he seems seldom to have fraternised with them or exhibited with them. He extricated himself completely from the restrictive aura of Irishness into a more expansive international scene. Choosing France as his adopted country, he severed his ties with Ireland when he sold off his inherited lands in Roscommon early in the twentieth century.

While active in France at the beginnings of modernism, O'Conor seems to have been much less conservative than other Irish artists of the period. William Leech, for example, was in Brittany in the early twentieth century, but his work captures none of the expressionist drive evident in O'Conor's paintings. O'Conor wanted to be part of the new developments, and though deeply influenced by a number of artists, he was in favour of independence and freedom of interpretation. 'Ignore the critics', he is quoted as having said, 'don't listen to them. Choose your own path and follow it.' This reveals him to be very much of his time. Post-impressionism, which could hardly be described as a style of painting, is little more than a facilitating label given to a group of individual artists who were exploring their own ideas after impressionism. Roderic

O'Conor, although not one of the innovators, was of this group.

O'Conor's subject matter ranges through landscape, figure painting and still-life imagery, with no one category dominating. It is in the landscapes, and more particularly the seascapes from the first half of his career, that he is most aggressively expressive, with a heavy use of impasto, and moving from a fluid, if exaggerated stripe-like application of paint to a jagged, *33* even choppy accentuation in the brushwork. This is certainly an exaggerated technique. While the impact is fairly dramatic, O'Conor seems to be making a very powerful statement about his commitment to the new developments in art. He makes use of a similar method in some figure and still-life paintings of the Breton period, but his later style, while remaining expressive, became more subdued.

O'Conor's continued reverence for old master painting and an echo of his early academic training reveal themselves in his constant commitment to the nude. If Velázquez is the name that most readily springs to mind in this connection, it must be acknowledged that O'Conor would also have been looking at the nude paintings of contemporary masters, notably Matisse and Modigliani. Occasionally his nudes are languorous, even inviting, but more often they have an inherent remoteness and seem to maintain the distance of the posed model.

It is in his still-life paintings that O'Conor appears a his most wonderfully varied. Using a great range o objects, such as fruit, vegetables, flowers and pottery, i varying combinations, O'Conor explores a number o different influences, from Manet, to Cézanne, to Matisse His sparse flower paintings have a gestural quality whic reveal O'Conor at his most passionate. There are als small, carefully orchestrated compositions, wit meticulous attention to texture. O'Conor makes muc use of a play of light in his still-life work, often settin his objects against the light; this leads to less immediat clarity and therefore a greater degree of interest.

O'Conor was never an abstract painter, and does no seem to have addressed the possibility of abstrac imagery, although this art style was being used lon before he died. Nevertheless, in some of his work h clearly manifests an interest in abstraction. Whil avoiding the minutiae of his subject matter, he becam more interested in the spontaneous, sketchy stroke o the brush, leaving decorative patterns loosely adherin to a drapery or a vase. The surface play of colour was i the end considerably more important than the reality o the object.

His lack of interest in abstract art is reflected in th absence of such work in his own art collection. I O'Conor's time it was quite normal for artists t exchange works, but he also purchased from dealers His collection comprised paintings and prints, and whil all of the post-impressionists were included, so too were the *Nabis*, Vuillard and Bonnard. There were also examples of the work of the expressionist Munch, and some of the *fauve* painters. Cubism and abstract works, despite the importance of colour in the latter, seem not to have found favour with O'Conor.

It has been suggested that Roderic O'Conor is Ireland's most significant painter of modern times. This has also been claimed for other Irish artists, in particular Mainie Jellett and Jack B Yeats. Although O'Conor was considerably older than either of these artists, their careers overlapped, with all three of them working in the first half of the twentieth century, and Mainie Jellett outliving O'Conor by just four years.

These three artists are very different, not just in terms of their art, but in relation to the whole development of their career and their subsequent influence. Jellett and Yeats maintained a strong commitment to Ireland but O'Conor unburdened himself of such a commitment early in his career, and his work therefore was not influential in Ireland. As an Irish artist working in a European context he may certainly be considered our first modernist painter, and as such, although many of his works are still in private collections and in Ireland, he is also well represented in international galleries, including the Museum of Modern Art, New York, and the Tate Gallery, London.

❧